THE BOOK
OF CROOKED PRAYER

poems by

Marcella Remund

Finishing Line Press
Georgetown, Kentucky

THE BOOK
OF CROOKED PRAYER

Thanks to the Women Poets Collective, for their invaluable help in shaping this manuscript, and for their generous and unflagging encouragement.

Thanks, especially, to my husband, Allen, for everything.

ACKNOWLEDGMENTS

Many thanks to these journals and anthologies for publishing poems from this
collection:

Action, Influence, and Voice: Contemporary South Dakota Women
Connoisseurs of Suffering: Poetry for the Journey to Meaning
The Flat Water Stirs: An Anthology of Emerging Nebraska Poets
Jabberwock Review
The New
Oakwood
Pasque Petals
Prairie Winds
Stirring: A Literary Collection
Switchgrass Review
The Briarcliff Review
Trees in this Neighborhood Remember Me
Typishly.com
Up the Staircase Quarterly
Without Fear of Infamy

Publisher: Leah Maines
Editor: Christen Kincaid
Cover Art: Joe Prescher
Author Photo: Marcella Remund
Cover Design: Elizabeth Maines McCleavy

Printed in the USA on acid-free paper.
Order online: www.finishinglinepress.com
                    also available on amazon.com

Author inquiries and mail orders:
Finishing Line Press
P. O. Box 1626
Georgetown, Kentucky 40324
U. S. A.

Table of Contents

Prayers of Desperation

*The function of prayer is not to influence God,
but rather to change the nature
of the one who prays.*

Søren Kierkegaard

Prayers of Supplication

ST. FRANCES GUMM

patron saint of girls who need to sing

Saint Frances, sixteen lifetimes of loss
spilled from you in a voice too big to hold,
echoed in the hearts of girls lost on stage,
rainbows tattooed on scooped-out pelvis
or small of the back. Nailed each night
to a marquis, you lived on spoonfed hosts
dipped in sorrow and sweat, just enough
to keep you thin, hungry, dancing at the speed
of light. Swaddled in organza and sequins,
humiliated and adored, you paved us a golden road
into the starlight—you, with hips too big,
crooked mouth made perfect in grownup red,
full lips teasing a mic (stand-in for men
who urged you on, filled you to bursting
with fairy dust until broken glass at your throat
felt like a kiss). Saint Frances, bring
the house lights down to hide my trembling joy,
keep me from back alleys, the bottle, the temptation
of dreamless sleep, the bite of a mic's metal
on my teeth. Bless me with songs like liquid,
songs that pump and clench my heart like a fist,
songs that soothe this radiant net of nerves,
songs that pulse in my heelbones,
cradled in rubies and glitter,
clicking for all I'm worth.

BLIGHT

i.

In the noisy oncology waiting
room, I blindly thumb through
Midwest Living. I see

instead the naval feud
in my mother's blood, cancer
cells conscripted to range

for food—marrow maybe, salt,
or tender organ meat.
Her lymphocytes

recruit, advance, retreat.
My mother is in a constant state
of half-mast, mourning

this war's casualties—
mother, brother, niece, self.
Back home she sleeps, electronic
ocean to muffle battle sounds.

ii.

Under a fat orchid leaf,
I find a sticky brown scale,
a she-mite's legacy, her

domed shield full of infant[try]
crawlers, her brood only
days away from colonizing.

They'll slip from their shells,
sail from leaf to stem to root,
their little scissored mouth

parts drinking straws for
Phalaenopsis sap, life blood
of my dying orchid.

Infiltrators. Usurpers. Always storming
the beach, always looking for a way in.
Dear god, what *are* we? Armies
or battlefields? Orchids or mites?

TEACUPS

I remember Aunt Elma's teacups.
I remember many tinkling teacups.
I remember them stacked, centered,
        settled on crocheted doilies.
I remember Aunt Elma.
I remember how she married a barnstormer
        (her sister married the barnstormer's brother)
        who drank his way across Iowa with The Babe.
I remember her son died in Poland during WWII.
I remember a heart attack took the other one, a daughter,
        after polio took the only grandchild.
I remember they don't paint *that* on porcelain teacups.

I don't remember the hairline crack
        in one blue porcelain cup, the crack
        that split in two the handpainted face
        of the Japanese woman, her gold-leaf
        collar, gold hands folded in her lap.
I don't remember how her split smile
        seemed to me, at four, a monstrous sad gash,
        or how the man standing behind her
        seemed lost in shadow.
I don't remember how the blue teacup threw itself
        from atop a tinkling stack of blue teacups,
        leapt at the glass door of the china cabinet,
        came undone and poured itself
        down over the bottom shelf.

Please, I don't remember Aunt Elma's teacups.

PRAYER TO A YOUNG GIRL PLAYING GUITAR

for Kaki King

The world has become
a spectacle of absence,
a radiant inventory.
                Christopher Dewdney

Because your pinafore is an alder guitar body shaped like a woman
Because your ringlets are shining rows of phosphor bronze
Because your hands are pale long-legged spiders dancing
Because your wrist bends back like the curl of a garden snail
Because your voice is small and high like a chipping sparrow
Because you call up Earth's low hum and it echoes in my ribs
Because you can disappear at will in a fog of sound or silence
Because you weave blue & silver chords into sheer electric fabric
Because your vibrato is a flame that trips nerves along my spine
Because you find a labyrinth of bright rooms in a glass bottleneck
Because you trick harmonics and women's fists unfurl, breath slows
Because old men cry and children stop fidgeting
Because ash settles lightly in the hearts of jealous men
Because these notes are an elemental baptism
Because you are hollow, a conduit radiating multi-tonal energy
Because when you stop there is only absence
Because 5000 people are fed, numbed, paralyzed
Because this is the sound a weeping fig must make
Because there was stillness and expectation and now this
Because somewhere in the desert tremors have begun underground
Because water bubbles up from hairline cracks in baked clay
Because yucca flowers open to nocturnal white moths
Because your radiance can be felt in the Kamchatka peninsula
Because day breaks into endless night
Because sixteen virgins weep and dress in black
Because I can only breathe, swallow, blink, wait

SUPPLICATION TO THE SUICIDES

for Ike

You will wake up tomorrow and the sun will be up.
            Stores will open. Some idiot will forget to signal
            his turn. There will be dishes to do. You'll get a job
            offer in Big Sky, Montana.
This will all get easier. Then it will get harder
            again. Then it will get easier again.
That girl you love will leave her next boyfriend too.
Your mother is canning peaches right now.
            She will need you here to eat them.
The pain you feel now comes from a cauldron
            of teenage chemicals swirling through you like bad
            soup, like toxic river water, like grain alcohol, like Drano.
            It will eventually push through your system, and you will
            be able to laugh and think straight again.
Remember that time I stomped in your house and screamed
            in your face and jabbed at you with my finger? I really
            wanted to hug you and lock you up and never let you go.
Going to the zoo is almost as much fun at 35 as it is at 13.
It will one day be a mystery to you that you ever felt this bad.
I don't know if there's an afterlife. But
            what if you have to watch the chain
            of sorrows you leave behind?
The belt will burn and cut into your neck. The pain
            will be unbearable before you black out.
            You'll pee your pants.
            You'll change your mind.
            You won't be able to stop it.
I love the way your hair flips to the side, and the way
            you look sideways when you grin, and the way
            my youngest son's heart opens up around you.
That girl you love will end up with four kids from three fathers.
            She'll work at Walmart and live over her parents' garage.
            She'll try and fail to kick meth. Her kids will be taken away.

Or

That girl you love will end up married to a banker
   and will live on a lake and have a housekeeper.

Or

That girl you love will be in therapy for the rest of her life.

Or

That girl you love will use your memory like a crucible
   in which she'll stew future boyfriends and cook up
   excuses for sleeping with her future husband's boss.

After your sister died, your mother stayed alive, in part, for you.

We are only here for a blink anyway. Can't you wait that long?

My son will have a redheaded child. She'll skateboard.
   She'll be beautiful and jolly and full of mischief.
   He'll take her to the skatepark in Lennox.
   He'll cry because you're not there to watch her.

You're my child. You're everyone's child. We will all be broken.

You'll fall in love again and again and again. You might have twins.
   They'll be skinny and blonde and hold your hand.
   You'll rock them to sleep with Jack Johnson lullabies.
   When they're 15, they'll say *we hate you.*
   You'll try to keep a straight face.

Your mother's smile will be manufactured and hard for the rest of her life.

You are so full of love and light and promise that it burns
   our fingers to touch you. We are moths and choose
   winglessness over being without you.

My son will carry you like a scar,
   like a confession,
   like a stone in his gut.
   Forever.

Someone will have to take a picture of your body.

There is nowhere else to go.

Please, please stay.

ST. DOMINIC

patron saint of choir boys

My sons, three wild choirboys,
have visions too, have wandered
in the fog, brilliant boys who catch
and sing the sun. Their high notes
burst like sparks against a dark
South Dakota sky. Their low notes
disturb the river's calm surface.
Teach them to settle disputes
as you did, with relics—
thumbs or long leg bones planted
in a tenuous line of truce, flag line
between their constant thieving
companions, Need and Want.
Bully them always toward
goodness & mercy.
Knock them down in the
schoolyard if you have to.

HOLY MARY MOTHER OF GOD

let them find my ex
and haul his ass into court
and get my rent money
let my landlord
keep his greasy hands off me
let me find a better job
than dishing up short stacks
at village inn
for 9-finger tom
at two in the goddam morning
let that piece of shit pinto
run one more winter
let my donny find his coat
in the lost and found
and start sticking up for himself
let me win the iowa lottery
so I can cover my bad checks at rexall
and that man tony from the quick lube on 42nd
       (not the blonde guy from the time out lounge on lake street)
let him be a good man
even if he leaves his boots on.

TOTEM

I am carving you into me, beloved—
totem, rune, petroglyph, icon, map.
Help me decode the world.

Paralyzed by the impossibility of
spinning planets or gravity,
I am only half, one ankle notched
with the easy way you carry wood
or level a cross beam.

Palms up, waiting for the red bloom
of sudden wounds or the hiss of air
from nailed tendons, I chisel
into a cocked hip the simple way
you love a dropped third,
a chord shifting to minor.

Crushed under the weight
of a hummingbird feather,
I cut into collarbone
the way you stake
trumpet vine,
gather bee balm.

I come to you,
you etched into me.

Teach me to love the ordinary.
Calm my fear of brevity.
Shield me from the cradle moon,
from all things too heavy with wonder
to bear.

PRAIRIE DARK

What draws us to the prairie is hard
and sharp as the blade of a paring knife
pulled through peach skin.

The faint yellow of kitchen windows
pools, thins to grey between
house, barn, gravel road

in darkness deep as a flour bin,
deep as apron pockets, deep.
Somewhere in the black

a cat carries week-old kittens
from a gaping cellar split open
to canning season

hides them in a tractor tire
overgrown with lamb's quarters.
Her ribs shift, glide,

a delicate cage where hunger paces
dark and beautiful as the shadow
crossing inside the kitchen window.

PULL OF THE MOON

My best friend Maureen slid
off the edge of the world.
Reverend Sun Myung Moon broke
her fall in a web of white gabardine,
set her down, descending angel,
at a wedding in Central Park.

She'd been falling for some time,
skin loose on the bone,
living on wild rice,
grapefruit, feverish
dark-skinned men.

The Reverend smiled east to west,
slipped brides and grooms
outlines of the apocalypse
as he rifled in their pockets for silver,
deeds, the occasional inheritance.

We've seen her since;
flesh full and round, laughing or
speaking French with a strange husband,
petting three olive daughters, and
once again drinking milk.

I HAVE NO PROOF

I have no proof that thirteen silver moons
crawl in orbits shaped like dented spoons
in bins of wayward silver left behind
when women pause, look up, and come undone.

I have no proof that planets sing—a prayer,
a breath, a minor scale, a sorrow thick as air—
like women hanging laundry on the line
who smooth a mended shirt and start to hum.

And this is how I think a world begins—
caught in a milky wash of love and pain,
a woman splinters, spins off and becomes
a glass mosaic earth, a tiled sun.

In deepest sleep, the coiled hours unwind
and we can breathe again, released, fine.
I have no proof and yet I know the sky
at twilight is a dark and half-closed eye.

ST. AMELIA

patron saint of girls who need to fly

I didn't mean to stop your heart
jumping spread-eagle like I did
from that ledge or the thousand
other ledges that tempt me
outside windows cracked
to let the cool air in
or to keep me from out there,
from St. Amelia

who calls my name,
an engine-hum prayer in the wind

> *ave khaos sancta khaos*
> *ave khaos sancta khaos*

whose beautiful boy's face grins
its patterns in the clouds
whose hymn is the clanging
of wings made of steel,
charts of the sky, iron bolts,
radio waves, cropped hair,
and longing.

We are running north and south
she cries.

and here I am again
creeping along another ledge,
waiting for an updraft.
She has blessed me with a need
to see things whole,
a back aching with the bud
of rivets and sheet metal wings,
a love of unreadable maps
and the nightly seduction of stars.

So I am sorry about your heart,
but St. Amelia is calling,
I am lighter than air, and

we are running north and south.

LETTER TO MY FATHER

It's four in the morning,
my skin warm against my husband's back
where I curve along his spine,
his breathing a chant.

I waited a few paltry decades for you,
this hole blasted in me
where your name echoed
in perfect rhythm with my beating heart.
You wouldn't believe the things
I've stuffed in there to muffle that sound—
bits of strung-out boys,
ancient incantations for the dead,
a shell-shocked drug dealer,
bark from a weeping willow,
apologies scribbled in crayon.

Do you know how many times
I peeled back my skin
to show you the color of my blood,
the way my lungs held air?
Late nights, drunk or stoned,
I'd sleep with my ear pressed
to the steel tracks, waiting for a sign
you were coming back
to say something.

Then one day you turned
in a stab of memory and I saw it—
the hole blasted in you.
We were only
what you stuffed in there, temporary,
all those awkward teenage angles,
never enough to fill you up
or muffle your own dark names.

It's quiet now.
Only a man's breathing—
that prayer, that song.

HERETIC'S PRAYER

I am outside, skirting the sanctuary.
It's true; I love your dark cocoon, air heavy
with frankincense. I look good in sackcloth.

I once swooned at Mary's alabaster feet, red candle
for each dead friend. But I'm outside now,
kicking gravel in the parking lot.

Father Church, middle-aged miser, you
stockpile tithes, real estate, paintings.
You pass off bleached sheep bones

as John's left thumb or Peter's anklebone
for cold hard cash, turn a blind eye
(under a gilded miter) from people

living on grubs. You turn goodness to sin—
peasant woman's pennyroyal to witches'
brew, harvest blessing to porn,

metaphysics to black magic, red-haired
night-owl Lilith to Adam's hysterical ex,
even Christ's own sweetheart to whore.

Uncover your ears. I'm wailing out here!
Tell me this is history. Tell me you've
dressed it down, wised up, that God's

army isn't still out there on horseback
hunting down blasphemers and heretics.
Tell me you've spread your arms

to the faithful women who've cleaned
up after you from the beginning. Tell me
your priest wrapped a pregnant, bone-hollow,

HIV-positive Sudanese girl in his velvet robes.
Tell me you've uncorked God's blessing, poured it out
for gays, divorcees, little boys lured

into the sacristy. Tell me your holy curator
bartered your stash of Egyptian relics
for rice and beans. Tell me you've gathered in

the lost chapters, turned your sacramental wine
to tears, pawned the fisherman's ring
for blankets, medicine, corrugated tin.

Tell me that late last night,
baptismal fonts ran with free milk & honey,
altars crumbled, roses rained from the choir loft,

Mary broke the rock, charmed the snake, wept.
Tell me *that*, and I'll come back inside,
fall down on my knees.

DEPRESSION AS SPIRIT ANIMAL

On a good day I see her only from afar,
grey wolfish blur curled against
the murky horizon. I look away
from the flash of her yellow
eyes—didn't that light once make
someone weep? I can just make
out her breathing, the rise and fall
of her great vague body.

On a good day I know (from gaps
in time or my husband's troubled face)
that once she had me by the scruff,
sank her teeth in, shook, pounded
me into the ground, snarled,
tore me to shreds. There should be
scars, tooth marks, pieces of ribs
that I could show you all.

And this is a good day. Today,
everything is painless, peaceful.
Who was ever caught in those fangs?
I half-listen for her soft pads, try
to forget/recall the shape of her eyes,
her rank breath. But she's a stranger
now—just a faint growl in my sleep,
a soft whimper now & then.

ROSARY

Holy Mary, where are you?
Holy Mary, full of whatever grace we will spare you.
Holy Mary, swaddle me in blue linen, cradle my head in your lap.

Holy Mary, lift up ten prayers for me, one for each time the world swallowed
    me whole.
Holy Mary, blessed with a broken heart, I too have sacrificed sons to the
    crucifying mob.
Holy Mary, blesséd are your fine white rib bones, on black velvet, behind
bullet-proof glass,
a five-minute peek for only $10 USD.

Holy Mary pray for us weeping penitents who, though blind, see that you are
too beautiful, too radiant—brilliant blue light on the cusp of burning
itself out.
Holy Mary, blesséd art thou among mop women, whores, pink foam curlers,
women who cut, red lace and whalebone bustiers, women with bruised
 cheekbones driving girls to school—uniformed girls who will one day
have their own daughters and their own bruised cheekbones.
Holy Mary, did you know even then the cord would become a fuse, would set
the world on fire, would lead Brother/Country/State to turn a cold
shoulder to Brother/Country/State, would be the rope we use to hang
ourselves, would whip neighbors into jackbooted armies waving
scalpels and embroidered silk bags of eyes & teeth?

Holy Mary, this is and always has been, the hour of our death.

(Amen.)

INVOCATION

If you were any more alive in me, Mother,
my heart would burst, split open
like a ripe plum soaked in holy water.

Whisper from every corner of this clapboard
cathedral, Our Lady of Perpetual Chores,
your small and powerful prayers:

> *white coral bells*
> *itsy bitsy spider*
> *battle hymn of the republic*

Chant caramel pudding and corn casserole
recipes, ancient sacred texts handed down
from your own mother, that dark marble saint

atop the bell tower, one arm wrapped around
a gilded laundry basket, a silver pressure cooker
cradled in the other. Her heart, too, burst open.

Keep me, I ask, in your blessing of trying, failing,
laughing about failure. Grant me the grace
of history, repeated mistakes, and promise.

Look down on me with love when they raise you
to the bell tower, at the way I sing your praises
off-key, from behind my daughter's stove.

PICTURE OF CHRIST

Dimestore picture of kneeling Christ,
lamb-eyed, purple-robed, hangs
above an old woman's bed—

a man whose long hair
might have brushed against her face
on moonless Nebraska nights,

whose petitions
might have soothed her,
healed her small, pale regrets,

whose sweet breath
might have saved her
from this dull cold of winter

and might have sung her
(fatherless, childless)
a psalm of satisfaction,

whose eyes might have
followed her, kept her company
on this desert of bluestem,

a man who might have wept
wine, honey, fallen stars
on the altar of her bare skin.

VESPERS

O'Neil Pass, Black Hills, South Dakota

The sun, luminous host of burnt orange,
golden rose, falls early into the open
mouth of the Black Hills. In shadow,
elk drink from a limestone sinkhole,
verdigris cup still running over
with Tuesday's sudden rain.
Bats wake, slip from pines still standing
or planed into cabin eaves, wings flutter
like paper fans in summer church.
Dakota skippers take one last blessing
from harebell or mariposa lily.
Whitetail doe coaxes a fawn up an aisle
of timothy grass to the sanctuary
of ponderosa pine, quaking aspen.
Dark settles in, stars blink on in the black
July sky, and then the singing,
invisible coyote choir at the treeline,
tremulous songs of love, fear, want.
Oh, the candles are lit, hymns echo
in thin, cool air—the priest is everywhere.
My heart splits like a wafer,
each caught breath my offering
on this plate of limestone,
and I am on my knees.

MALA

In the beginning was the breath,
inspiration exhalation illumination.
It was and was not,
a strengthening pulse, becoming,
stirring up salt and clay
in a deep cauldron of stars
pitched to one side and spilling
pale light, liquid invocations
into thin air—

> *ohm mani padme hum*
> *ohm namah shivaya*
> *our father our mother*
> *Saturn Mercury yin yang*
> *nameless spirit who unifies heart and mind*
> *mitakuye oyasin*
> *tanzih tashbih*
> *St. Jude thin ray of hope*
> *grandfather grandmother*
> *Jahveh I Am That I Am*

and the breath shaped its perfect
full mouth around the Word
formed us from three elements
set us down in the fourth, fire of the Word,
let us play and burn for ten-thousand years
making oblations in the fire
tears wine sperm tears blood
let us tease spark from vein
and hold it against our skin

until cinders worked their way beneath our nailbeds
until flame licked the bone
until spark curled up in the belly
until the only heat was in the belly
until the air was cool and dry
until the ground went cold

until we understood flame and ash
until we sat naked and shivering
until the rain fell.

Pools formed in indentations
footprints of wandering gods
and on the slick surface of the water
we saw ourselves, clumsy, too fat
or thin, aching and wounded
we saw each other only in that rippled mirror
eyes cast down and fixed
on an image of our own bluing upturned hands
so delicate so hypnotic that we

would not cross the water with a poultice
would not set the bone
would not speak the Word
and darkness fell.   In the blackness
silhouettes against a pock-marked moon
we pushed and pulled the muck
into mountains snowcapped and treacherous
until fenced in, we came to adore
the dark and silvered mirrors

distorted images of bent knees, sloping backs,
small breasts, muscled thighs.
We formed our small trembling mouths
into awkward shapes
stood half-erect with heads tilted
filled our lungs with air
filled the air with only hoarse wavering
grunts and hisses
could not fit our mouths around the Word.

This earth, this pool, is the cracked mirror
in which we are still caught as
ten thousand planets heat and cool

ten thousand stars blink to life
scatter, explode in the watery night
while we shiver, naked,
dim shadows against a cave wall, mouthing
the Word that would release us
the Word we clamp behind our teeth.

In the dark, in the cold
in crags or on sudden plateaus we strike
blindly at rocks, dig at the root
but always make our way back to the water
back to our selves
rippled and silver in brief glints of fog or moon
broken when the breath moves the Word
across the surface of the water
where we lean in, locked in a long gaze.

And sometimes we hear it,
the perfect Word skimming the water, pushing up
along the rock faces, drifting into gaps with a sigh
a beautiful sad tremolo
that clashes in dissonant chords
with cries from across
a distant mirrored pool
brackish now, encircled in a white salt ring,
our temporary crust of light.

> *ohm mani padme hum*
> *ohm namah shivaya*
> *our father our mother*
> *Saturn Mercury yin yang*
> *nameless spirit who unifies heart and mind*
> *mitakuye oyasin*
> *tanzih tashbih*
> *St. Jude thin ray of hope*
> *grandfather grandmother*
> *Jahveh I Am That I Am*

make my jaws unclench
make my fists uncurl
make my heart split open like a ripe plum
make my arms reach out over the water
make my eyes look up from this illusion
make my silver blood pour out over the ground
make my lungs fill to bursting, my mouth round,
help me make the sound, the only prayer, the Word—

   LOVE

SPIRITUS IMMOBILES

Think—

of a migrating bird's hollow bones,
snapped against a bitter crosswind,
or the latticework of ancient porches
splintered in a sudden prairie gale,
or a field of corn, stripped to confetti
in a flash of hail.

Think—

how a foot slips the precipice,
the long fall to ponder the long fall,
or the sudden seize of a heart, breathless
wait! wait! on the tip of a blue tongue,
or the car wheels' slow glide on black
ice, the guardrail a suggestion, and

how do I dare

put one foot before the other,
brush my hair, wave to the neighbor?
How do I put on my coat, when
that thin line looms so near,
listens for the creak of my door?
You feel it too. How do we dare

go on?

KINTSUKUROI

for Alison

When it all breaks apart—like
your young daughter, whose breast cancer

transforms her into a Picasso
of hollows, misplaced & missing parts,

this face's angles less sharp above
her husband & children in foreground,

that face pulled into a tender, finite point
so close we feel it needling our skin—

you begin to know there is no
real mending of fragile things,

not your teacup nor your daughter,
not your heart nor this broken life.

There is only the constant
filling of cracks with molten gold

(gathering family, well-meaning friends,
the rank perfume of flowers,

another casserole, another day), until
the golden seams make the cup

both delicate and stronger, until your cup
holds water again for a moment, until

you see, maybe only
for a split second,

something shiny there,
something worth saving.

Prayers of Illumination

WAITING IN EREBUS

Here in Erebus, frigid waiting room outside the gates
of Hades, a water cooler gurgles. On the wall, a 1966
NASA calendar. A shifty-eyed Kit-Cat clock ticks
its tail. From somewhere, *Goin' Down Slow* plays
on repeat. We drum fingers on the arms of vinyl
chairs, our fingernails brittle and methylene blue.

Teeth clacking, we sneak glances at one another,
guess by mark or remainder the falls
that brought us each here: a lit match, husband's
belt cinched around his two-timing neck, lover's
cliff-diving shove from behind, icicle driven
through the soft parts, bad breakup with a timber axe,

hands pocketed when we could have lent help.
We, the undutiful and indifferent, the decomposed
& disarticulated, don't look back. We thumb
through *People,* cross and uncross our bony ankles,
suck on Lifesavers, wait for our names to be called,
for a door to open, for that first blessèd blast of heat.

COOLING

It is evening.
I am running my fingers
along the glass curve of you, beloved,
and thinking how like a bead of silica
we are in the fiery beginning,
and how, with a perfect aperture
and a long slow breath
we are set spinning
in someone's careful hand.
A molten bubble
spinning, then weighted
to one side or another,
bulbous   and beautiful   and still
a spinning translucent something
until a base takes shape,
a groove, a lip,
the turn of hip and handle.

Tonight, as I touch your smooth glass surface,
I know the terrible secret—
that even a molten center cools,
comes clear.

PUSHMI-PULLYU

We are born astride the grave,
someone said, and so it is we're
taught from birth to live in fear.

Pushmi-pullyus that we are,
we stand guard, one eye (or two)
watching in a 360° pivot, the less

splendid gazelle in us perhaps watching,
while the unicorn in us sleeps,
relaxed in its ancestral magick.

Such clever design, never turning
our backs on all we fear: sounds
in the dark, silence, ominous wind,

owls, inauspicious numbers, the color
yellow, each other, ourselves, dust,
love, rejection, death, no death.

HOUSE OF NO SOUND

I live in the house of no sound
where footsteps are muffled somethings
and even my breathing is shallow.
A song I once sang prowls outside
under frozen hydrangea
caught in mid-bloom,
like the song's gaping mouth
pressed now against my window.
Inside,
not even boiling water
breaks the silence.

ST. THEODORA

patron saint of the displaced

Mother Theodore, how did you scrape
the sweet dark French from your tongue,
turn your back on the emerald sea, scale
the crags to roll stones against the mouths
of salt caves, sail across a bluestem prairie
to the brackish ponds of Indiana woods?
How did you bite off the heavy English,
mouth full of fat earthstars plucked
from under tulip tree mulch? How did
you find your way out of the woods
those shadowed mornings? I have only
sticks and twigs, a web stretched above
the spurge, the empty page and broken
binding of a fallen pin oak, an offering
of moss, this aching to fall on my knees.
Come back to the woods, Mother,
give me your iron heart, your faith
like a pressed habit, your smooth
white fingerbones to tuck in my hem.
Lead me out of this strange dappled light
where I hide among gooseberry thorns,
cut and quaking, clinging fast to the ivy.

FRAILTY

I sing the sorrow of temporary beauty.
O breast, slope in the small of the back,
arch of foot, pendulous earlobe. All of us,
faulty mechanisms by design. Ball and socket
rusted to lead, vocal cords like vibrating
hummingbird wings, singing their own
demise, disappearing sperm and egg.
We are sand mandalas, masterpieces
admired and brushed away.

I sing the despair of the human body.
If these bodies are vessels to house
radiant energy for a time, waves
and particles that will spark beyond
the crumbling of these clay jars,
then surely the body's poor design
is the atheist's manifesto. What intelligence
would craft a slowly dis-integrating
barrel in which to house a beam of light?

MOCHAJAVA IDYLL

Brackish water cooled in sunlight
I wake chanting to the dark beast   humbled
a chicory garland twisted in my hair
walk the coals to the kitchen
where you sit
cup cradled in your hands so tenderly
time grinds to a snaked unwinding
we lick our lips while we
boil   and boil   and boil
hungry for that melding moment
we circle the Circle
sink   to stove   to table
and the linoleum crawls with lichen and fern
our cool bare feet wearing a groove
until we're ecstatic   fertile   singing

mochajavakenyasumatra
mochajavakenyasumatra

and we dance the dark dance
and we drink the black oil
again   and again   and again
until we fall redeemed
into moon and moss
the big dipper spilling black
into a saucer of sky

RESSURECTION

I dreamed our missing peacocks came home,
waste-thin from shelterbelt or dry creek bed or
wherever they'd holed up, driven from our farmyard
by desperate badger, coyote, turkey buzzard.

I dreamed the drought hadn't starved us all,
hadn't picked raccoons clean, hadn't dried & bleached
bones white as salt flats, hadn't vaporized
pastures and turned wisteria to grey dust.

I read that Homer's spirit fled into a peacock.
I dreamed my spirit lives in them too,
in their vague Phoenician promise
that I'll rise again from this ash heap of a life.

I dreamed they all came home. They fanned
their tails, and Argus' thousand sea-blue eyes
saw me resurrect (misshapen, scorched)
from the burn pile, crawl off toward water.

MUSE LIKE CLINT EASTWOOD

Rough me up. Be indelicate.
Go ahead, spit. I want the brief
brutality. You think a ruffled
hem, the faint perfume of lilies,
or eyes like dark half-moons
will push this lazy pen?
Don't coax; shove. Send me
off the cliff. I need to feel
the impulse when ground slips
from under me, when the cold
indifferent air turns its back
on me. No cooing or cradling.
Lean over the edge, chew
the butt-end of your stale cigar.
Sneer. Call me a whiny little girl.
Wave goodbye. Look bored and
walk away. Trust me, that'll get me
clawing at the blank page of sky.

ST. ANTONIO MARIA CLARET

patron saint of those who lead mediocre lives

Saint Antonio, both father and mother,
fire of holy love, we have come to see
your heart, that living furnace of eucharist,
valves still flush with sacramental blood.
What can you teach us now, the lost
whose suffering is to smolder but never to burn,
whose poverty *siempre, siempre, siempre*
kept you awake as a child, put the scourge
in your teenage hand, drove you to wander
from your books out into the sea,
your lungs filling with salt, until *la Virgen*
plucked you from the water? Weave us
answers, threads of skin or hair the warp & weft
of a luminous tapestry, blazing constellation
of winged boys on whose backs you were lifted up,
carried over frozen rivers or countryside
buried in ice and snow. Saint Antonio, the
sacrament still blushes in your red heart—
let it spark us, the weak-spirited, into fire & flame,
we who choose not to choose, our own blood
too thin, too slow, too far from the hearth,
our lives a constant cooling, cooling,
cooling to pale blue in the drifts.

HOW TO PRACTICE POETRY

Take a long walk.
Breathe deep.
Taste the air.
Keep your eyes open.
Try not to think.
Wet your lips with your tongue.
Tilt your head slightly into the wind.
Separate the sound of single stone
cracking under your boot.
Feel the difference in weight
between a milkweed seed and a blackbird's feather.
Stray from the road on your way home
until you are waist high in wet corn.
Approach your house from the back.
Whistle for the dog with the white mark
like a crescent moon on his chest.
Look your children in the eyes when they speak to you,
and raise your eyebrows, and smile when they smile.
Notice your son's mouth curves up on one side,
and his fingers are long and squared-off at the tips like his father's.
Search your daughter's right heel for the star-shaped scar
where they tapped her for blood when she was two days new.
Drop everything when your husband gets that soft, glazed look
and presses his palm into the small of your back.
Think to yourself how like the spreading roots
of a silver maple
are his hands.

ST. JOHN OF GOD

for David

What if there is no dreaming, no dancing,
no opalescent mist in which we float
suddenly weightless or winged,
what if trumpets don't sound
and in no distant fog
do chords come clean from harps,
what if there never were seraphim
swallowed in flames of love
so radiant we turn our heads?

What if there is only a pause
a mirrored moment in which we see,
most of us for the first time,
our selves, and in that moment know
with certainty that we have been bathed
in love since the beginning
that all along while we wept and prayed
saved unanswered letters
left the receiver on the hook

we were pure love twisted into human
shapes so, like impulse and receptor cell
we fit, and could only spark together,
tendon and bone going up in a flash of love
so radiant people turned their heads?
What if that moment is all we have,
one gauzy white curtain drawn quickly
over a small dim window then
out, out, into the long night?

St. John, was it looking out too soon
that drove you mad, or could you bless
me with that moment now,
walk me past the mirror now,
with the window still wide open,

curtain billowing like a sail until I
know love, love, love, that sea
of flame and beautiful sorrow
so radiant I turn my head?

LETTER TO NIETZSCHE

I hugged a horse near Devil's Slide,
fell to the grass, not afraid
to bear terrified silent witness
to the union—dark, seamless—
        of Nothing and Nowhere.

Between a rooted spear of grass
and me, a stronger will has grass—
driven to constant, glorious growth
even as the blades approach—
        a fine-split hair.

The grass alone may rise above
good and evil, lust and love.
I'll buy bower land for Death
amid the pulsing prime of health—
        God's steady, slow decline
        in perfect parallel with mine.

BOOK OF THE DEAD

On the third night,
two comets converge
with a lunar eclipse. We kneel
in the twigs and ash, press
our vision into microscopic
spaces between stars.

Out of blackness
an explosion of pinpricked light,
sparks released at last
from the heat of resisting gravity,
freed from bodies going cold,
fanned through a million
crown chakras in a chant
resolved at the edge of a galaxy
in a single sustained note.

For a moment, sparks glitter
everywhere then funnel
into the dark, pulled
along a path
of dust and flame.

We close our eyes,
make grieving love
in smoldering leaves,
burn our own gash
in the black breathless night—
       la i'llaha, il Allah hu.

ST. JOHN THE BAPTIST

patron saint of health spas

Let me burn slowly in the fire
of Midsummer, feed me only
roast lamb and hypericum,
let me sweat off a pound a day
for forty days and forty nights,
wrap the demon cellulite clinging
to my thighs in a pall infused
with kelp, salt, lemongrass,
let your dizzying mineral steam
drive out this ghostly evil adipose,
stir ashes and dust into rosewater,
a fine holy paste for stubborn heels,
purge these wanton open pores
with fennel and warm clay, anoint
my idle hands with castor oil and lanolin,
lead me beside distilled waters
(my ass will need a miracle).
Let me fit, at last, into that black
crepe dress, the slinky one with
blue glass beads like fading stars,
the one I keep buried
in my cedar chest.

ANGEL

Where my shoulder blades angle out and away,
I feel budding wings, pinfeathers still tight
in their waxy shafts. And if I would only rub my back
against a fencepost, hollow bones would pierce the skin.
I would tilt into early morning sunlight and the shafts
would split, wax flaking off like early snow. A gust
of northern wind would blow scapular feathers
into perfect barbed intersections, while I hunker down
in the pasture, waiting for coverts, secondary feathers,
(at last) flight feathers. I would arch forward, stretch
wings over pale clumsy arms, wings open and tipped
in feathered hands. I would fold and unfold
the new wings, run my teeth along waxy spines
to pull each feather into place. If only I could shake
off this dark weight of earth—anomaly of amygdalae
that makes bones too dense, melts disappointment
into leaden veins, carves anchors of loss and sorrow.
If only, in a sudden updraft of impossibility, these wings,
prehensile and tucked near my heart since birth
or before, would make sudden graceful figure eights,
would scoop air and push it back in undulating
cushions of lift, just maybe, I would fly.

BRONCHIAL LOVE

March 31, 2005

Midway through 104-degree
delirium, I wake briefly
in sudden profound joy
to the certainty
that John Paul and I,
bed-bound feverish brethren,
are steeped in a mind meld.
We drift away.

Illuminated in scarlet,
weightless now,
we pirouette
in a breathless dervish,
lungs laboring in thick air
above a blue fog chasm
that separates the living
from the dead.

Stunned by the
silence, the grace
of our dance, my clever
thoughts hang in blue blue blue
air, a useless bridge.
I grin my schoolgirl grin
and he names me
Only Love.

Two days later my fever breaks,
he whirls on without me.
I click back into clever
and must not speak of this,
how I know I've been sick,
how I know I've been cured
above a foggy precipice
by love, only love.

THINGS I NOTICE ON A SUNDAY EVENING

Beloved, there's something strange about the way you feel
tonight, your new pulse slower,
less demanding.

Along the length of your arm the hair is finer than before,
brown silk over a pale blue web spinning itself
just under your skin.

Where the curve of your back sweeps my hand out,
down the plane of your leg to a sloping foot,
bones become delicate.

I see you from odd angles, the concave of throat,
the hollow behind an ear, the rich landscape
of hip and thigh.

You look strange in this light. Has there always been
an east window in this room? Have you been leaning back,
watching, since before I came?

It all means something now—every slow rise,
every careful shift from one foot to another, every pause,
when I feel you new-born, old for the first time.

ST. PLACID

patron saint invoked against chills & drowning

Face up,
under the weight of water
black and cold as empty space,
my body spreadeagle,
pressed into a silt angel
like a child's handprint,
ringed in black diamonds, these
bits of million-year-old carbon,
I watch for you—
for that Heavenly spark
that could show me the surface,
send its warm current
deep enough to make me
weightless.

ST. WILLIAM BUTLER

patron saint of midlife

Like you, I love to watch the lithe young girls
glide along the walk, their bellies a striptease
of what's to come, their hips, those swinging
pendulums of time, breasts like water wicks.
Or shirtless prancing boys all undulating muscle,
pants sliding down inverted pyramids, greenwood
frames already drying in the sun's kiln. But we,
caught between kiln and cane, are wrapped
in good hard living. This layer left over from
childbearing, that mound a testament to the
healing magic of cream & wine, feet splayed
from a million miles of chasing the unnamable,
breasts already halfway in the ground, muscles
gone to folded flesh. In teashops we vacillate
between dying animal cells and rarified wings,
hovering, weeping, between hell and heaven.

SATELLITE

It's all about reception—

The way ponderous insects the size of your open hand
couple on twigs thin as air
in a clash of knife-sharp mandibles;

the way heavy birds balance on water,
half-drowned in a wet tango,
fan serrated feathers against a fall;

the way big cats stalk sex,
crouch low, lick the air for musk,
flex claws like switchblades.

the way you turn toward me,
bounce your signal off the inside of my thigh,
up my spine and out across this summer night.

Prayers of Desperation

RELIC

I keep this shard in my pocket,
cut glass to remind me of you,
how you came near once,
dim blue light refracted
in a broken cup I refused,
rapt in my own skin,
my eyes unfocused or closed,
and how I felt you hold on,
tenuous grasp on whatever
footing I would spare you,
etching yourself in me,
and how the flutter of you
sent a spark up my spine,
tripped me to sudden weeping
or laughter, and how you left
then, a vapor trail across
the dotted Milky Way,
and how sometimes in sleep I watch
your eyes open, know you know
I couldn't risk your soft breath,
and so I carry on as if you'd never
come, though deep in my pocket
I finger blue glass knowing
it will split the skin like birth,
knowing blood will soak the seams,
knowing you are the pale light
of a minor constellation now,
or the impulse in
someone else's sudden smile.
I finger blue glass and feel
the bite of you. It leaves a bruise
like an open blue eye.

DESTEMMING

Let's cut the stems from all roses,
so that without the risk of blood,
we can inhale—undeterred, piggish,
insatiable—the sweet perfume.

This is the way of things now;
excise whatever gives us pause.
Scrape off this too-thin skin,
shut these eyes that won't stop

seeing, plug ears that hear
whimpers, scoop out the heart,
that traitorous bundle of beats, strip
nerves that could spark something.

And when the world plucks us,
petal by petal, we will finally be
bald and painless heads—mute, dumb,
so smooth, so full of nothing.

ST. JOAN OF ARC

patron saint of the impossible

What were you thinking, 19 years old,
lashed to the tree as good Christians stacked
dry kindling shoulder high? Did God
whisper in your ear *then*, to make you smile
that way, your eyes rolled back, muscles released
in ecstasy or terror, and lift your breath in what?
a sigh? a gasp? And when the torch bit, was it
God's hot kiss that made you, pillar of fire, press
from your lips a French hymn even as your lungs
compressed, oxygen too having given you up for lost
in a wilderness where even the sword melts away?
And near the end, could you see past waves
of heat, eyelids seared open, sackcloth stripped
from your naked body smooth as a young boy's,
to the English priest swooning on his knees,
hands moving under cassock, could you hear
his hushed, private prayer, his undying gratitude?
> *O, that God had given him this gift to offer up
> on an altar of flame, the One, the only woman
> worth the hell of love!*
And where had you gone, when afraid of your lingering
spell, they pulled your heart—red, perfect—from the ash,
the gravel of bone, and tore it into harmless pieces?
St. Joan, forgive my frozen faith, this icy petition.
Burn your mark in me, my skin so pale,
so cold to the touch.

TRIPTYCH:
BODY, MIND, SPIRIT

Mother

This panel is the Madonna,
whose hands have pared and cut
bitter onion, turnip, carrot,
whatever meat could be found,
have sealed it with salt, water and fire,
have buried day-old kittens,
necks snapped by a restless tomcat,
have peeled back the burnt skin
on a child's open palm,
handprints brittle and delicate
as silvery flakes of mica,
have scrubbed stains from
a girl's rose-patterned bed sheets,
have traced invisible, holy signs
on the skin of a man's back,
have followed the curve
of his muscled hip,
have folded around him in prayer

Daughter

This panel is the Magdalen,
who once lifted her foot to step over
a fallen tree branch and stopped
mid-air, caught in a rippled vision
of a tree from which the branch
might have fallen, then the constant
inescapable drip drip dripping
cascade of incessant thought—
a scored, moss-covered trunk,
thick wandering branches,
spreading fan of twigs,
intricate lacework of new growth
suspended in air, tree and not tree,
or what space there is between,

or the nature of Tree, her Self
at the root—She, Tree, Air, God
and Water, always Water

Fire

In this panel, pain,
myrrh, desire, and rainwater
burn clean, constant.

TRIPTYCH:
THE NATURE OF FLOOD

This is the nature of flood—
a woman pauses a split second too long,
conjures a face beloved,
a soothing voice,
the taste of a lover's mouth,
forgets the water is waiting.
A thousand hairline cracks blow open
in the deep sigh of this moment,
terrible and clear as any river.

The prairie is cut by the hard-edged river,
black water cold as underground.
Water moves inside, too,
in a clapboard house
where a woman huddles in the corner
of her kitchen, rocking on her knees.
It's the middle of an endless night.
She's backed against the cupboards,
half smothered in a dishrag
to muffle her cries.
She wants to breathe.
She only wants to breathe,
stomach muscles twisted
into tight pincurls.

Under the bald eye
of the Moon rain falls, rivers
open to the sea.

TRIPTYCH:
RURAL SCENES

In the howl of an angry month, it's best to build
something. Knee-deep in quicksand, set posts
of bent forks, paper walls with newspaper & spliced
magazine covers (doe-eyes facing out), chaw spit.
Consider carefully the placement of furniture—hide-a-bed,
gun rack. Cover blast-hole windows with flour sacks,
heirloom tablecloths, burnt bedspreads. When the thing
is finished, this sinking thing, back out, watch the door
for signs of life. In a better month, they'll drag
the sticky quagmire, find these things we build.

We occupy space, vaporous, silent,
moving about in the background,
pressed like dried coneflowers
beneath unrelenting burdens.
We bless and curse and please you,
split ourselves open at the seams for you,
mending mending mending
what we have not torn.

Out in the thicket
wild plums burst in summer rain,
too full of moonlight.

STUCK ON RED

A beat up Ford pickup barrels past,
two heads bob in rhythm.
I'm stuck midtown at another red light,
constructing their story:

The boy is 17,
all wide mouth and feed cap brim,
maybe it's Corn King,
because he is that royal,
sleeves rolled up on a t-shirt
so white it lights up the dash,
one tan arm hung out the window,
the other invisible,
steering with his knee.
Maybe it's his uncle's pickup.
Maybe it's the middle of August.
Maybe he's supposed to be sacking
groceries at IGA.

She's 15, pressed against him,
riding the gearshift.
She smells like jasmine or lavender.
She brushes the back of his neck
with her braid
in a move she picked up
from MTV.
Her hand is in his lap.
Maybe her dad's the police chief.
Maybe she's really that blonde,
pink skin so hot
it burns his fingers.

She flips her braid to one side
and disappears.
          gone   gone   gone
and so is he.

GIVE ME THE CRUMBLING BODY

Bodies are not made to last. We are flimsy
hinged dolls, our hollow motors
shut down by faulty wiring or love.

One wrong move and a bone snaps, an eye
goes milky, explosions blacken a brain.
All the right moves and still a cell splits

sideways, sparks a civil war, dis-integrates
lungs, bladder, breast from the inside out.
Outside, the expansion & contraction of sun,

rain, wind, jealousy, and disappointment,
leave roadmaps of spider cracks and fissures
where fog creeps in and youth seeps out.

But I will take this temporary housing,
this body broken and crumbling to dust,
over one of rivets & steel, its ungrateful,
tin heart ping-ping-pinging forever.

THE IDES OF MARCH

The seer was right to warn us,
beware the ides of March.
It's a dangerous time, peering
through iced windows at the jeweled
tease of crocus and daffodil.
We've weathered another season
of deep-freeze, locked up tight
in muscle and mind. We're tired
of winter's grey and gritty leftovers.
But this is no time to get careless,
toss a floorboard heater through
the beveled glass and go out,
where Spring flashes her flannel petticoat
embroidered in pinks and greens,
leaves us gaping, breathless
in air still cold as a knife blade,
stripping off the down.

GRIP STRENGTH AS EXISTENTIAL LITMUS

Marian is patient with the therapist.
She's tired today, she says. Ready to go.

She's going to a better place
she says, where Jack is waiting.

He'll be so relieved—he never could
take care of himself.

She sees it: They'll settle in for coffee,
zuchini bread, *Let's Make a Deal.*

This isn't a promise, or a hope, a testament
of her faith. She is *dead sure.*

She knows it as she knows the constellation
of liver spots on her arms,

as she knows what Jack is doing
this very minute—renting the wrong

heavenly bowling shoes, or putting his cup
in the wrong side of the heavenly sink.

She's still smiling as she lets her arm go
limp, refuses to lift and lower the ball.

I reposition my own lazy hand, squeeze
the grip strength tester for all I'm worth.

MARTYR

When after fasting and prayers
he blows a policeman, 12
schoolboys, and himself to bits,

he will dwell eternally in the land
of milk, wine and honey,
will see Allah's sweet & smiling face,

will join brothers, uncles, cousins,
will have his sins erased,
will rest, his head forever pillowed

in the laps of black-eyed, perpetual virgins,
his devoted wife somewhere nearby,
having taped C4 discreetly

between her cloaked breasts, one last
cellphone call away from breast, wrist,
thigh, upper arm, all a living rain

showering a marketplace, so that she
will be allowed to stand upright at last,
will be allowed to stand eternally

behind the husband who for 33 years
pressed The Law, his unyielding
stone tablets, into her back,

will be allowed to give thanks
for her suffering, for these martyrs'
blessings. And who are we, Bibles
and rifles in hand, to judge such gifts?

ST. DYMPHNA

patron saint of the mentally ill

Dymphna, in fitful dreams I find you shivering
in rowan and ferns along the Blackwater
river, wreathed in St. John's wort
& anointed with yellow rattle,
half starved and wrapped in a celtar
cinched at the waist with an oak rosary,
humming strains of your mother's brief
lullaby. But your father was a chieftain
and knew the magic, found you anyway.
Grief or madness drove him to finger
your small bones for signs of her
in the curve of your emerging breasts,
the winged cup of your pelvis, your
silky down, and you a fugitive
child with courage enough to keep locked
that garden gate, though he found you
again, sealed the gate forever. Forsaken
daughter, in my own trembling delusion
I am your *Síle na Gigh*. We offer up
a novena to our Mother and for nine days
I give you this blessing too—my stone lap
cushioned with heather & moss, pillow
for your bruised and worried brow.

EVOLUTION

This is the beautiful secret,
that women steer toward the shallows
in midlife, leave behind the fierce deep
where young gills, those fresh wounds,
fan in punctuated pink bloom.

Such secret women angle off,
slip out of the river, creep
onto dry land in the cool evening.
Scales lose their glimmer, harden
into a delicate skin of pearl.

Suddenly the lungs! A quick gasp,
then breathing steadies, rises and falls
in rhythm with dry things: earth, rock, sky.
No longer a darting flash of silver,
such women move deliberately,

their plodding grace and practical
cold beauty like the water itself.
On the riverbank, they lift
onto sturdy legs, shiver in new air,
set off in every direction.

Some take to the hills, curl into
dirt floors of caves, keep
to the shadows, live on lichen
peeled from damp cave walls,
cry over shallow pools in the dark.

Some gather in threes or fours
in the woods, build fires, fashion
bowls from fern and sphagnum,
cook rich stews to buoy
the newly-legged women.

Some cartwheel into the open,

prance naked in meadows
or weave among cornrows,
laughing, dizzy, hysterical,
alone at last with this stranger, Self.

Some go back to the water,
try to swim with their ponderous
split fins, those legs. These women
sink to the murky bottom, where they
call like sad, netted sea creatures.

Best to keep moving, moving,
keep to the dry land, keep
to the company of rooted trees,
coneflowers, sundogs—keep
to things that cannot take you down.

HOW COULD YOU KNOW?

Mid-month. My body has turned
on me again, another cauldron
stirred into a roiling, gulping boil.
I'm idling at frantic,
each nerve ending in spark,
skin a smooth bed of fire,
and this constant hunger.
Yes, I loved you yesterday.
But today, all the world is flameflameflame
and you lie here, cool and grinning.

EVANGELIST

Each time Epiphany flips her switch
and my pulse quickens or my eyes blaze,
I run headlong into an Evangelist—
see the soles of his bare feet, feel her
breath on my neck, let him inside.
Each brief visit, I trip on a wagging
fiery tongue, fall from the even landing
of grace, have to start the climb again.

Sometimes he's middle-aged, jittery,
a tray of stiff collars in his lap.
Or she's teaching Spanish, *sígame,*
bobbing wimple, hands tucked away,
black patent shoes shining under
a rough habit. Sometimes he's leaning
under a streetlight, so rare, so beautiful
that my heart pours out, holiness
spilling down a storm drain.

My first slip was birth, jarred loose
from drowsing in a cradle of luminous
cord, shot down the human slide
into the blinding antiseptic world,
my mother straining on the altar.
The gloved Evangelist chanted verses
from the *PDR*, teased out my first
confession, that gulp of air, with a scalpel.

I slipped again at ten, Twin Brooks Bible
Camp, where little girls were tucked
like pink seeds in rows of old streetcars
planted across the Nebraska prairie.
Starlight jogged my memory and I confessed.
I'd be back, I said, not willow tree
or sad-eyed cow but a better me,
dark haired, maybe a ballerina.
At breakfast, the red-faced Evangelist

took the mess hall stage, led his flock
in prayer that shook rivets loose,
amen and amen, for the fallen girl.

> *And then a dream, god's soft familiar*
> *voice, reminding me not to waste the rinds*
> *of fruit, kumquats maybe, in a wooden*
> *bowl on a wooden table, in a small angular*
> *attic. Simple, the two of us chatting, light*
> *streaming in a small round window.*

Another fall outside an Omaha head shop,
picture of teen drama in my black
wool cape, on the prowl for black candles,
incense, *Llewellyn* charts, a black
cat asleep in the shop's bay window.
The Evangelist crossed the street waving
a neat chart of the Apocalypse. She took
my wrist, her eyes rolled back like dim
saucers, a hiss escaped her teeth
like steam, like a black cat.

Late spring in Berkeley, he found me
on stone steps near a fountain where
African drummers called up the water.
Dressed in sackcloth and sandals, wrists
braceleted in heishi and dried apple seed,
he kissed me, said he dreamed I would
come then turned away, crossed
the square singing a hymn of oceans,
waves of somnambular love.

I married him once, each day a little
purgatory trapped at the kitchen sink
as he offered up his litany of terrified,
righteous warnings—scrub this, scour that,
cover those milky breasts, their rose stars,

that constellation that drives holy men
into the rocks. Each night he counted
birth control pills like prayer beads,
placed one gently on my tongue
without a blessing.

> *And then god again, walking with me*
> *under a wooden arch, carved letters*
> *spelling out "les enfants," strolling like*
> *two old friends. So easy, that soothing*
> *voice in my ear, something about the way*
> *French rolls like blue water off the tongue.*

I saw the Evangelist last in a classroom,
sweatered, bearded, baskets full
of ancient verse and slippery meter. He kept
one foot in the doorway, eyes fixed
on the seductive distance. He gave me
the fine agony of words, laced with his
low drone: *everything you want*
is somewhere else. Run, run.

But today I saw clouds, greys brushed
with pink and orange in a perfect
cursive V across the tissue paper sky.
Geese scattered their staccato notes,
the quarter moon a tilted signature,
and fields of winter wheat,
my soft green landing.

FIST

for Jonestown, Heaven's Gate, Solar Temple, and the rest

God—the fingers of his right hand
grown together in a fist above his flock—
could not have lent any help.

Not when a thousand lambs
invoked his thousand names,
hoed an empty path,
kept vigil in a barren garden,
nor when finally starved
and cast out they gathered
eyeless needles, dipped their magic
hopeful wands into poison,
not when the first child's face
blued, when mothers
drank their loss to sleep,
when fathers lay beside
their drifting families.
Not when a thousand
fragile lives spun out & away,
iridescent, brief as comets.

Somewhere in my fitful sleep
God weaves a mud-brick road home,
calls me to uncurl my hands.

EXEGESIS, BOOK OF WOMEN

Examine the historical underpinnings
of this open book of women in cotton leggings,
before that rubber garters in metal clips,
flesh-tone nylons cinched and chafing
an inner thigh, wool stockings before that,
and before that linen pantaloons, all the way
back to bare legs. What can it mean,
those legs locked around a lover's waist?
On this page the image of a figure 8,
on that page the consonance of weeping
in a spotless kitchen, at the back an appendix
of near accomplishments, footnotes
throughout, losses so deep they can't be
plumbed here, each chapter a re-made life
in the catch-and-release of making & unmaking
women, a final index of slights, miseries,
rare & hoarded joys, the paper itself a metaphor
for the thousand skins women peel away
or layer on, and always, always,
a dedication to tired, thick-veined hands
that will someday write their own book.

SHE IS NEVER ENOUGH

She is a testament, a monument
to the comforts of her kitchen,
to bad meds, faulty joints,
too much breast milk or not enough,
to corn and soybeans, long, still winters,

to slow metabolisms, abusive fathers,
friendless childhoods, romantic betrayals,
media conspiracies, patronage,
to wild gene pools where breaded, pan-fried fish
swim in currents of heavy cream.

O, the potlucks, where her breasts,
those banners of bulk, announce her arrival.
Where, even as she reaches the table
with a Velveeta and tater tot masterpiece,
parts of her are still arriving.

O her thighs, their friction sparking
brush fires in the grass. She, a walking,
delicious, backyard barbecue. O her footsteps
or dancing, tribal rhythms
that beat our hearts for us.

Let us celebrate the plenty of her,
the enfolding, the enveloping,
the subduing of glass-sharp angles
and uncomfortable jutting ribs,
the quashing of size 2.

Let us give thanks for the cornucopia of her,
overflowing abundance and radiance,
her body in constant undulating motion,
her beauty too splendid, too generous
to fill only one cup.

LETTER TO ST. JOHN LICCIO

patron saint of head injuries and strokes

Dear (St.) John,

When I could first form pictures again,
I pictured you weeping as my brain imploded,
as fire burnt through the cord between my brain
and her circling planets (eye, arm, ribs, leg, foot),
all spinning out & away,
          cut loose from the sun.

But I heard you were playing cards in a strip club
at the time, waiting for a slip from the stage,
as my dying black-hole neurons sucked in stars.
Ten times a day I repeated my own name,
nurses kept me tethered
          with needle & meds.

When I got home, you were busy counting
car crashes, football tackles, trampoline falls.
I was learning to live without gravity,
to button my own shirt, shower, sing,
find my nose with my finger—
          my left foot still lost to me.

But I can work miracles too, John.
I lift up my eyes to *neuroplasticity,*
Forget walking on water, fishes & loaves,
mended prostitutes, incorruptible
hearts or livers. Sew up
          your magic bag.

St. John, ghoulish ambulance chaser,
I'm sending out a new cord, twisted lines
of memory, old photos, stubborn will,
a catalog of prescription drugs.
I won't need *you* to turn this supernova
          into a brand new galaxy.

BODHISATTVA

My mother's cancer is in her blood,
mercurial cells jumping their vesseled
banks to tributaries of lymph, spilling
tumor seeds in lungs, breasts, brain.

Mercury comes from the Greek
hydrargyros, "water silver."
Its atomic number is 80, of course,
same as my mother's.

In Tibet, mercury was thought to mend
broken bones. Alchemists used it
to turn base metals into gold.
And maybe that's all true.

Maybe the water silver in my mother's
body is mending someone else's bones—
my mother is like that, always fixing
someone's broken wing or heart.

Or maybe it's turning the base metal
of her traitorous body into pure
golden energy that when released at last,
will pulse through us, out into the ether.

We are never ready.
And maybe this is her first and last
lesson for me: Water silver, like
everything else, must return to its source.

MANDALA

Mandala, yantra,
map of the hidden world,
chart of the heart's constellation—
we are born in your center
and with our first breath scrabble out
to the edges, where we navigate emptiness,
pillage and expose to the sweltering sun
the nothing out here, our skin sloughing off.
We have nowhere to go but in.

Sometimes muscle memory or despair
pulls and we creep back toward you, grope
along vine-covered walls on hands and knees,
muscle and bone wired together
with coaxial cable and speaker cords,
our pulse digital, our eyes a matrix
of dimming pixels. Again, we get it wrong,
drag with us the din of signals sent or received,
echolocation of fear, manufactured fog
against our own reflection. Somnambular,
paralytic, hollowed-out, we ride shockwaves,
drift away from ourselves,
away from the heart's deep metronome,
away from the center's pinpoint stillness,
away from Love's dark labyrinth,
away from the only divine number, One.

Mandala, tantric lens through which
we could finally glimpse ourselves,
we've never had anywhere to go but in.
Light the way to your radiant center.
Light the way to your angular private rooms
bathed in cobalt, saffron, magenta.
Light the way to your bed of roses
where, if god is anywhere, It is here.

MARCELLA REMUND is a native of Omaha, Nebraska and a South Dakota transplant, where she teaches at the University of South Dakota in Vermillion, directs the University's student literary organization, the Vermillion Literary Project (VLP), and coordinates a community writing group.

Her poems have appeared in numerous journals and have been selected for prizes by journal editors and by judges including Odilia Galván Rodríguez and Molly Peacock. *The Book of Crooked Prayer*, her first full-length manuscript, won Honorable Mention in the Stevens Poetry Manuscript Competition from the National Association of State Poetry Societies. Her chapbook, *The Sea is My Ugly Twin*, was published by Finishing Line Press in 2018.

Marcella is busy on her second full-length collection, poems based on the Magdalene laundries of Ireland and the U.S. and on her recent travels around Ireland. Marcella and her husband live in a multi-generational, multi-species home in South Dakota. You can keep up with her at www.marcellaremund.com